Let's Finish the Picture

To Parents: This activity builds spatial reasoning skills. Call attention to the characteristics of each piece to help your child complete the picture.

Sticker

Cut out the animals at the bottom of the page.

Glue each one to its matching ☐ .

Let's Trace Curved Paths

To Parents: This activity builds handwriting skills through practice with gently curving lines. Have your child use a pencil or crayon to trace the dots.

GOOD JOB!
Sticker

Trace the ▩ ▩ ▩ from ➡ to ➡.

Glue   Glue   Glue   Glue

Let's Color the Picture

To Parents: In this activity, your child will practice finding the differences among colors and shapes. Encourage your child to color within the lines. This will build fine motor control.

Color **red** the areas that contain a ○. Color **brown** the areas that contain a △.
Color **green** the areas that contain an ✕. Color **blue** the areas that contain a ☐.

4

Let's Trace the Curves

To Parents: This activity builds handwriting skills through practice with many different curving lines. Encourage your child to stay on the gray dotted lines.

GOOD JOB!
Sticker

Trace the ▪ ▪ ▪ from ➡ to ➡.

Let's Circle Ocean Animals

To Parents: Ask your child to name each living thing (whale, mouse, fish, horse, squid, chicken, elephant) on the page. This activity helps your child better understand the world.

Find the 3 animals that live in the ocean. Draw a ◯ around each one.

Let's Color the Flowers

To Parents: Ask your child to name all the colors he or she uses. This helps to build an understanding of the differences among colors.

Color the tulips using any colors you like.

Let's Glue the Animals in Place

To Parents: Here, your child will exercise his or her fine motor skills by gluing pieces to a specific place. If your child has difficulty reading the animal names, read them aloud.

Cut out the animals on the bottom along the gray lines.
Glue each animal to the ☐ next to its name.

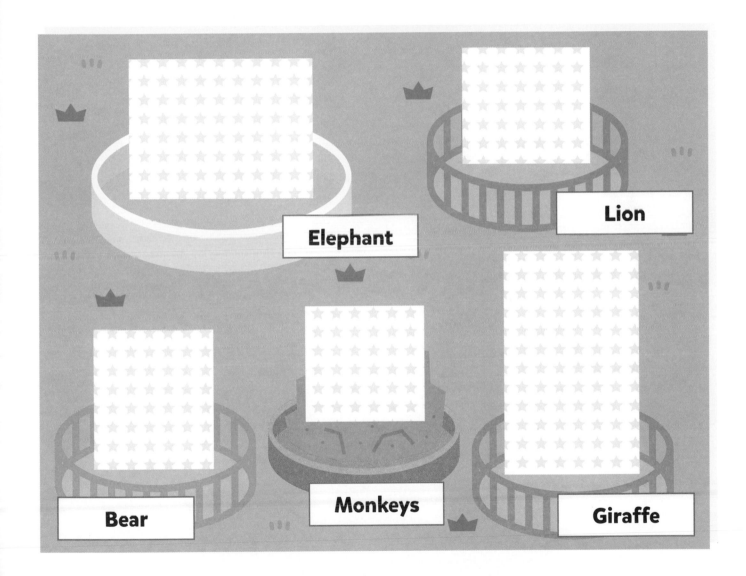

Elephant

Lion

Bear

Monkeys

Giraffe

Let's Trace the Loops

To Parents: This activity builds handwriting skills. Encourage your child to go slowly and trace the overlapping, curving lines carefully.

Trace the ▦ ▦ ▦ from ➡ to ➡.

Glue

Glue

Glue

Glue

Glue

Let's Draw Matching Pictures

To Parents: This activity builds handwriting skills while encouraging observation. Ask your child to pay attention to each example picture to see which dots should be connected.

Draw lines between the dots to make pictures that match each example.

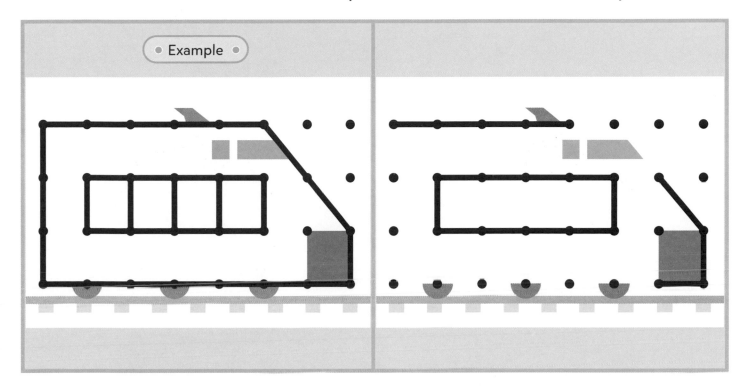

• Example •

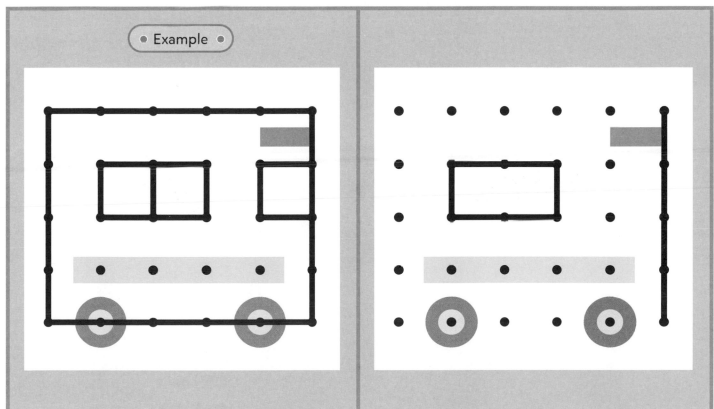

• Example •

Let's Practice Being Polite

To Parents: Here, your child will practice manners that are used when dessert is served. Use the stickers in the front of the book. Ask your child what to say when asking for dessert and what to say when dessert arrives.

Sticker

What should you say in these scenes?

Apply the sticker that matches each scene.

When you would like dessert

Sticker

After you have received dessert

Sticker

Let's Feed the Animals

To Parents: This activity helps your child better understand the world. After finishing the activity, ask your child what other animals like to eat.

Find the food each animal likes to eat.

Draw a line to connect each animal with its food.

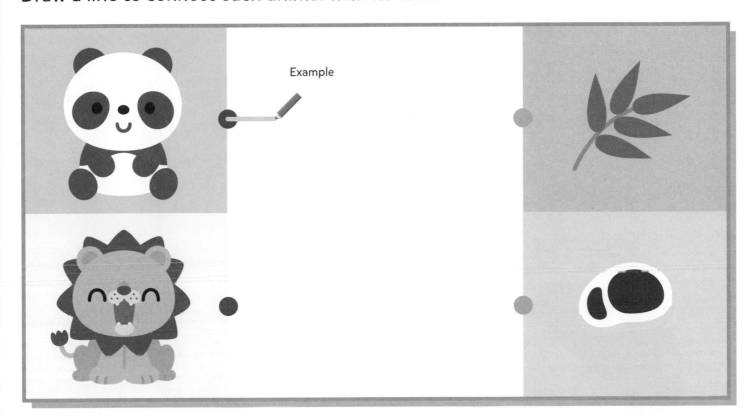

Example

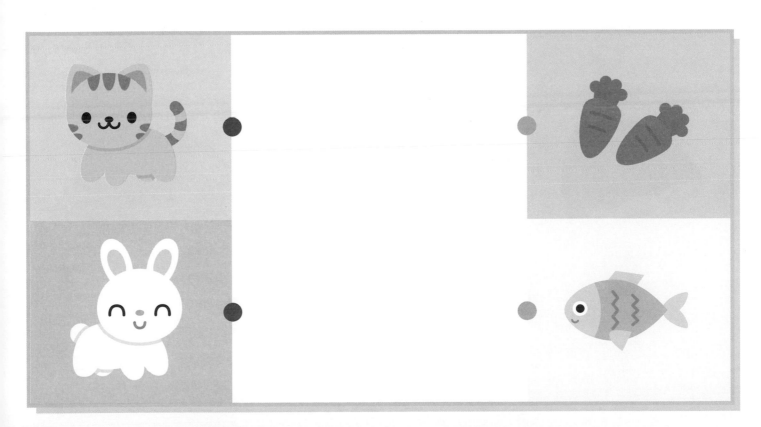

12

Let's Find Matching Umbrellas

To Parents: In this activity, your child will practice spotting the differences among objects. Encourage your child to cross out the umbrellas that do not match to keep track of the ones she or he has already checked.

GOOD JOB!

Sticker

Find the 2 umbrellas that match the example.

Draw a ◯ around each matching umbrella.

Example

GOOD JOB!

Sticker

Let's Build a Robot

To Parents: Cutting and gluing help to build fine motor skills. Call attention to the direction of the robot's shoes and ask which one is on the right and which one is on the left.

Cut out the robot parts on the bottom along the gray lines. Glue each part to a ▢ to complete the robot. After gluing all the parts, use the stickers to finish the picture.

• Example •

14

Let's Find Matching Kebabs

To Parents: Here, your child will practice identifying the similarities and differences among objects.

Find the 3 kebabs that are exactly the same as the example.
Color their ◯. Then, color the fires.

Example

Glue

Glue

Glue Glue Glue

Glue

Let's Match the Shadows

To Parents: Guide your child to look at the shadows first to determine the match for each animal.

Draw a line between each shadow and the picture it matches.

Can you make the sounds each animal makes?

Example

Let's Draw Spots on a Giraffe

To Parents: Find a picture of a real giraffe and show it to your child. Explain that your child's picture does not have to match the example or the picture you showed. Encourage your child to be creative.

Draw spots on the giraffe.

Example

Let's Remember the Picture ①

To Parents: This activity exercises memory skills. Go over the different kinds of vehicles together during the 20-second period.

Look carefully at the picture. Try to remember what you see.
After 20 seconds, turn to the next page.

Let's Remember the Picture ②

To Parents: If your child struggles to find the differences, have him or her go back to the previous page and start again.

Find the 2 differences in the picture from the previous page.
Draw a ◯ around each difference.

Let's Find Hidden Numbers

To Parents: In this activity, your child will practice finding hidden objects. It might be easier for your child to find the numbers if you divide the picture into sections or search each object (tree, house, curtain, etc.) one at a time.

Find the numbers 5, 6, 7, 8, 9, and 10 hidden in the picture.
Draw a ◯ around each number.

Let's Connect the Dots

To Parents: This activity builds an understanding of numbers while improving handwriting. There are arrows from 1 to 5 to help your child find the next number in the sequence. If your child has difficulty with the higher numbers, offer help.

GOOD JOB!

Sticker

Connect the dots from 1 to 20 in order.

Let's Find Matching Leaves

To Parents: In this activity, your child will focus on the similarities and differences among objects. Because the direction of the leaves in the picture is different from the example, your child must pay attention to shapes and colors to find the matches.

GOOD JOB!
Sticker

Find the match for each leaf in the example box. Draw a line to connect each match.

Let's Find Animal Homes

To Parents: This activity increases your child's understanding of the world.

GOOD JOB!
Sticker

Where does each animal live?

Draw a line to connect each animal with its home.

Example

Let's Play a Cooking Game

To Parents: Children often enjoy games based on food and cooking. Help your child follow the instructions below. Encourage your child to have fun. Cutting and gluing exercise fine motor skills.

GOOD JOB!
Sticker

First, cut out all the objects below by following the gray lines.

● How to Make ●   ★ "How to Play" is on the next page.

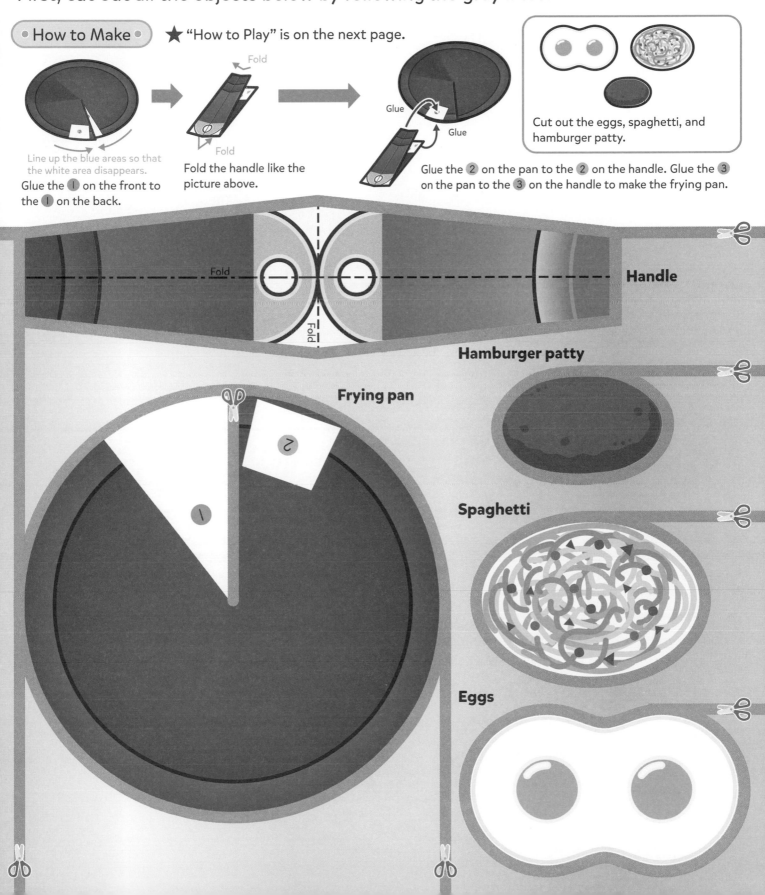

Line up the blue areas so that the white area disappears.
Glue the ① on the front to the ① on the back.

Fold

Fold the handle like the picture above.

Glue

Glue

Glue the ② on the pan to the ② on the handle. Glue the ③ on the pan to the ③ on the handle to make the frying pan.

Cut out the eggs, spaghetti, and hamburger patty.

Handle

Hamburger patty

Frying pan

Spaghetti

Eggs

• How to Play •

Put the hamburger patty on top of the frying pan.

Flip the hamburger patty by moving the frying pan up and down quickly. Try to flip the eggs and spaghetti, too.

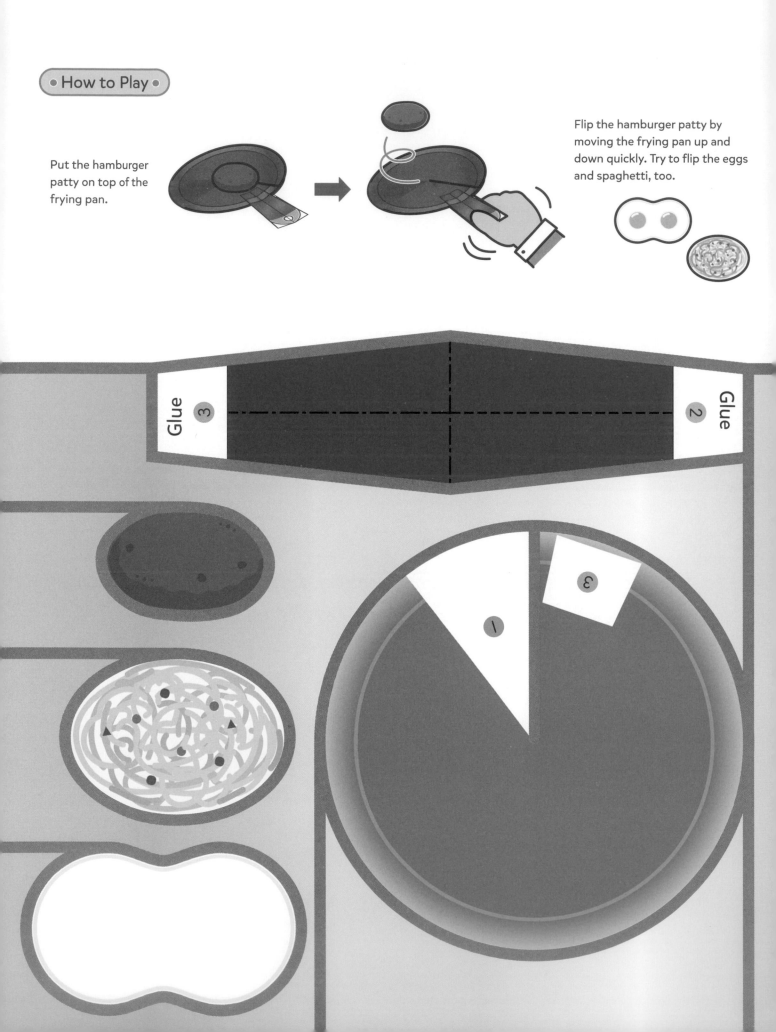

Glue 3

Glue 2

Let's Go Through the Maze

To Parents: Your child will use reasoning and problem-solving skills to get through the maze. Ask your child how many apples the squirrel gathered all together.

GOOD JOB!
Sticker

Help the squirrel gather apples. Start at the and count all the apples along the way to the ➡.

Let's Go Through the Maze

To Parents: Mazes exercise problem-solving skills. Guide your child to find the shape (diamond, heart, star) on each gray box to see where to put each envelope sticker.

Help the mailman deliver the mail. Draw a line from ➡ to ➡. Along the way, apply the mail stickers that match each [Sticker].

Let's Find Matching Shapes

To Parents: Call attention to the different characteristics of each shape to help your child find the matches.

Which shape on the right matches the one in the example?

Find the matching shape and draw a ○ around it.

Let's Follow the Animals

To Parents: This activity builds problem-solving skills. Ask your child to name each animal in the maze.

Draw a line from 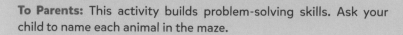 to 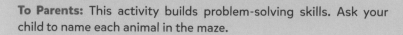. Take the path with only animals.

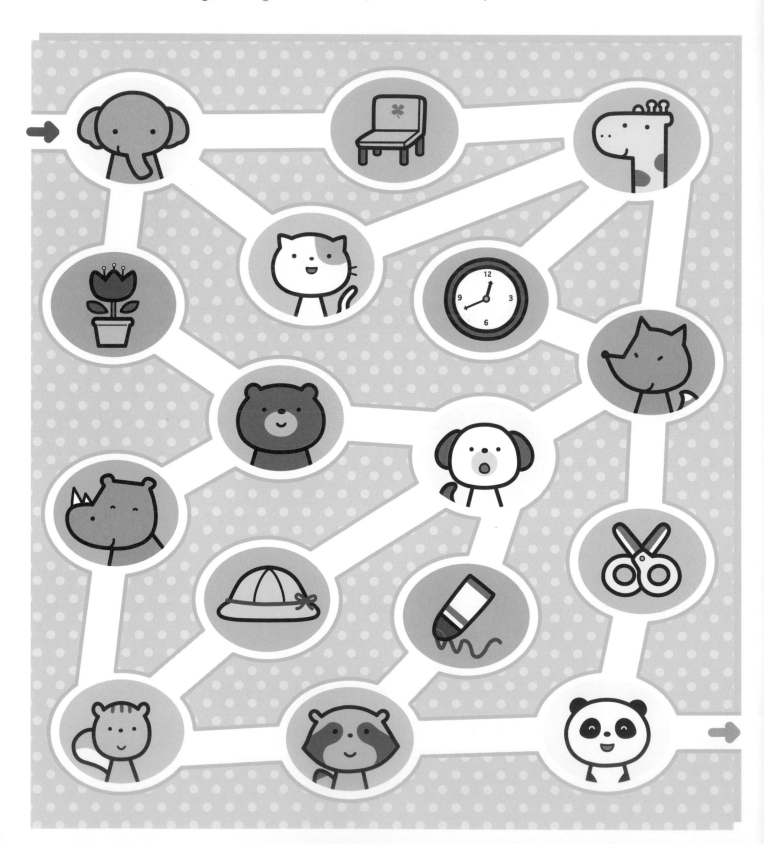

GOOD JOB!
Sticker

Let's Glue the Animals in Place

To Parents: Here, your child will exercise his or her fine motor skills and reasoning skills. This puzzle combines a cut-and-paste activity with a part-to-whole matching activity.

Cut out the animals at the bottom of the page.
Then, glue them where they belong in the picture.

Let's Match the Shadows

To Parents: Call attention to the details of each shape to help your child determine which shapes match.

Look carefully at the shadows on the left. Can you find the shape on the right that matches the shadow? Draw a ◯ around each matching shape.

Example

Example

Example

Glue   Glue   Glue   Glue

Let's Draw Matching Pictures

To Parents: This activity encourages attention to detail and builds handwriting skills. After finishing the activity, ask your child to compare the drawing to the example to check for accuracy.

GOOD JOB!

Sticker

Draw lines between the dots to make a picture that matches each example.

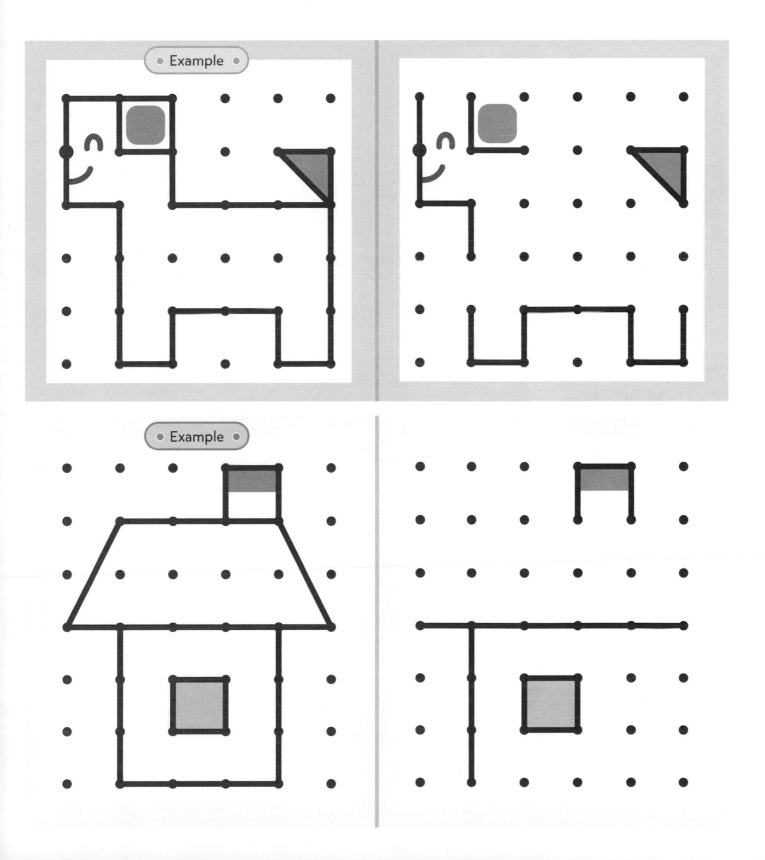

Let's Put Events in Order

To Parents: Putting events in sequence builds critical thinking skills. Ask your child to describe what the person is doing in each picture. See if your child understands that the pictures go in order.

Compare the pictures on the left and right. Which one happens first?
Color in the ◯ below the answer.

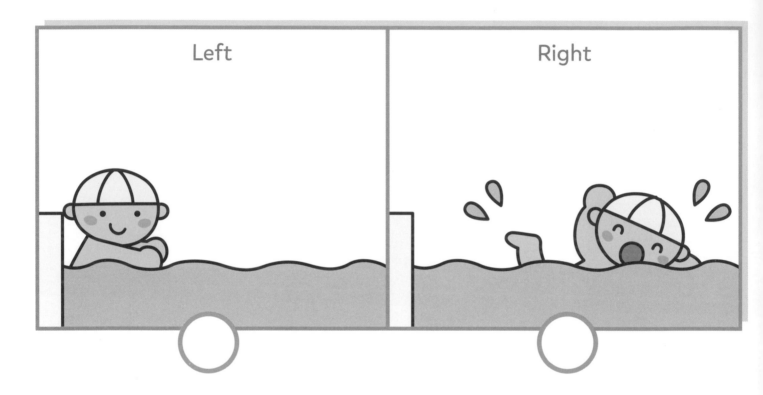

Left | Right

Left | Right

Let's Find What Doesn't Belong

To Parents: This activity increases your child's understanding of the world. Ask your child to explain why she or he chose each answer.

One object in each group does not belong.

Find it and draw a ◯ around it.

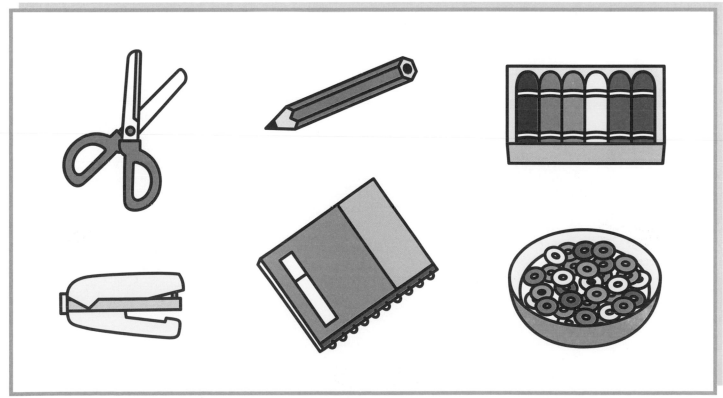

Let's Make a Pattern

To Parents: Here, your child will practice putting things in order to make a pattern. Help your child see how the items alternate.

Look at each row. Something is missing. Which object comes next? Choose a sticker for each 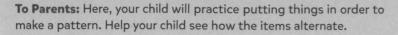 to complete the pattern.

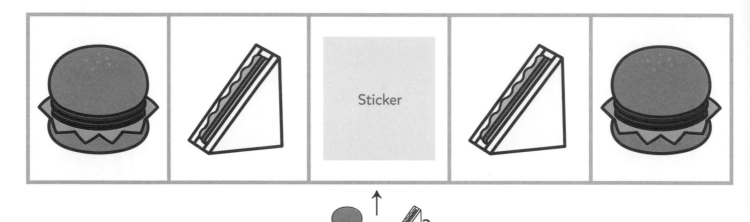

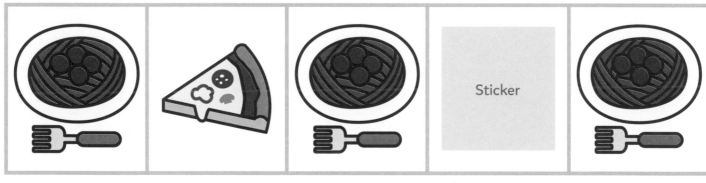

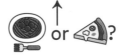

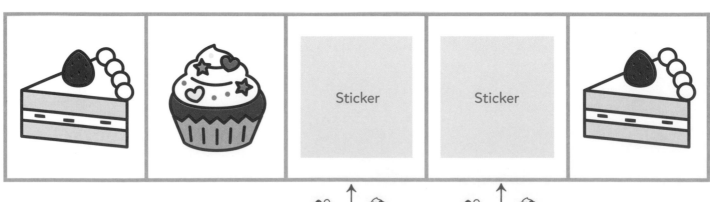

GOOD JOB!
Sticker

Let's Make Puzzles ①

To Parents: This activity builds spatial reasoning skills through making and playing with puzzle cards.

Cut along the gray lines to make puzzle pieces.

• How to Make • ★ "How to Play" is on the next page.

Before

Cut along the gray lines.

After

Let's Make Puzzles ②

To Parents: Play with both sides of the cards. Have your child match the pieces by looking at the pictures and by fitting the shapes together.

GOOD JOB!

Sticker

• How to Play •

● Match by Picture

Match 2 pictures halves to complete an animal image.

● Match by Shape

Put 2 shapes together to complete a rectangle.

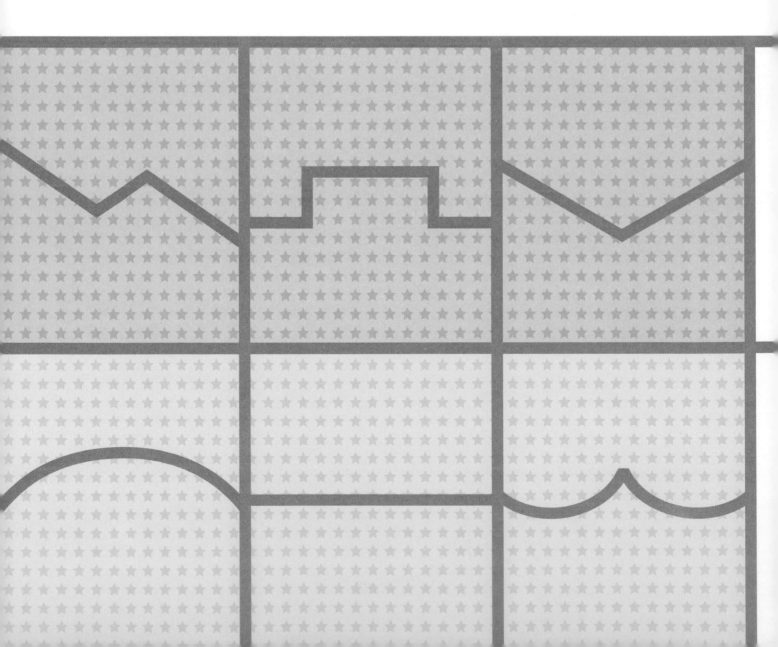

Let's Make a Pattern

To Parents: In this activity, your child must recognize similarities in objects and then put those objects in order according to a pattern or sequence. Have your child say the names of each fruit out loud (apple, melon, banana).

GOOD JOB!
Sticker

Cut out the squares at the bottom of the page. Glue each piece of fruit along the path from ➡ to ➡ so that it will be in the order of .

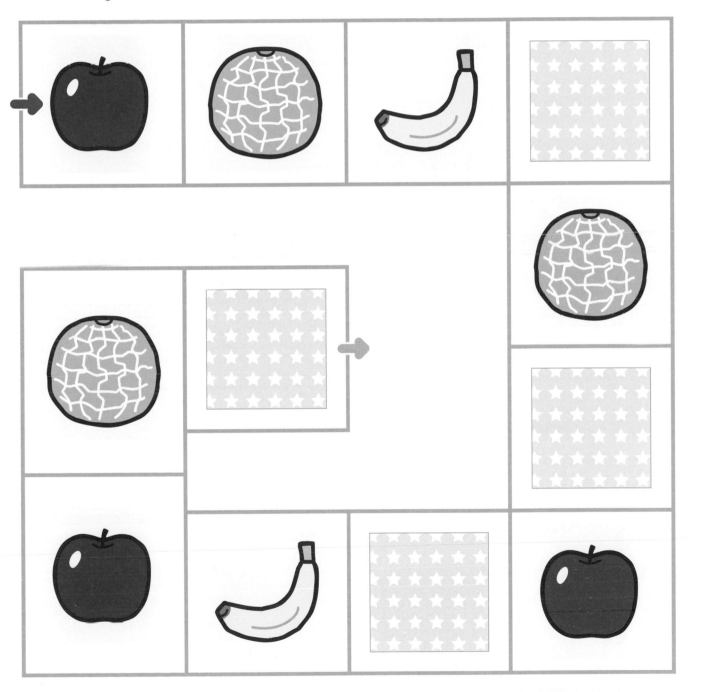

Let's Learn About Seasons

To Parents: The activity helps your child better understand the characteristics of each season.

What season does the picture show? Find 3 items used during the season in the picture and draw a ◯ around each one.

Flip-flops

Straw hat

Scarf

Mittens

Swimsuit

Warm hat

Inner tube

Glue   Glue   Glue   Glue

Let's Guess How the Food Is Cut

To Parents: This activity builds critical thinking and problem-solving skills. Cut actual fruits and vegetables vertically and horizontally to show your child the differences.

GOOD JOB!
Sticker

Look carefully at the examples. How do you cut each fruit or vegetable to make it look like the example? Color in the ◯ by the answer.

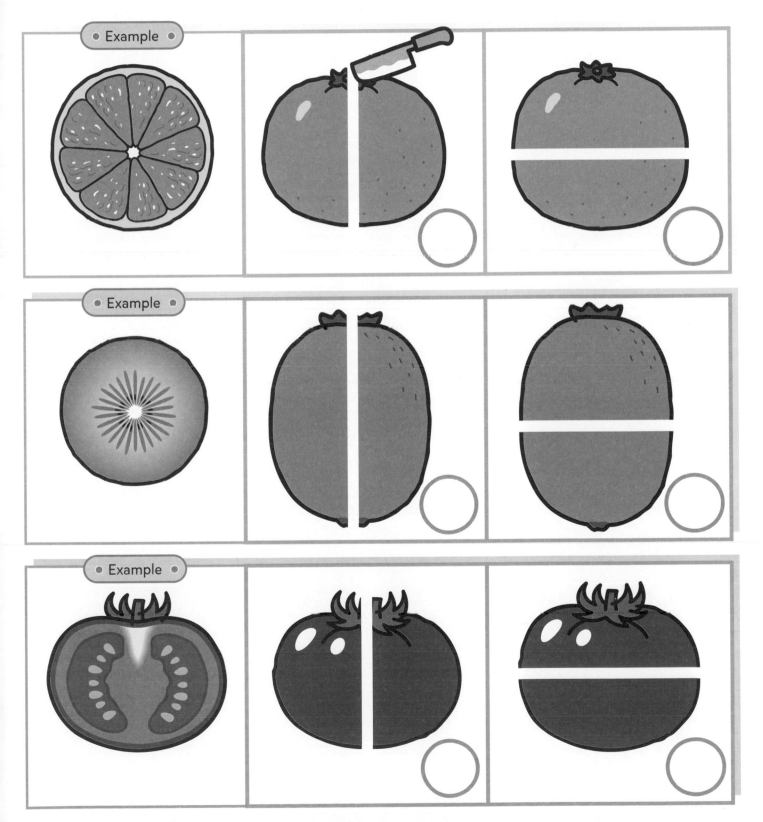

Let's Find the End of the Maze

To Parents: This activity exercises your child's ability to look ahead. It is also a maze based on "The Three Little Pigs." Tell your child the story after he or she completes the maze.

GOOD JOB!
Sticker

Draw a line from ➡ to ➡ to complete the maze.

Let's Match Animal Shapes

To Parents: Here, your child will practice using shape and size to match pictures to their shadows.

Cut along the gray lines to make animal cards. Which sea creature matches each shadow? Glue each card to its matching ▢.

Let's Compare Sizes

To Parents: In this activity, your child will focus on size differences among a group of similar objects. Emphasize the color to be used in each task to help your child remember when to use red and when to use blue.

In each box, color **red** the ◯ below the biggest item and color **blue** the ◯ below the smallest item.

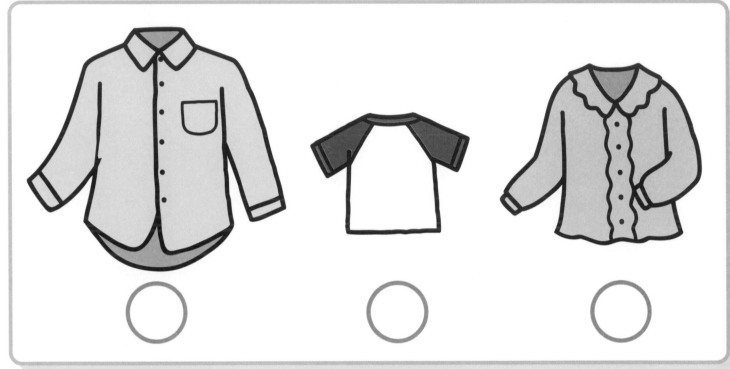

Glue   Glue   Glue   Glue

Let's Remember the Picture ①

To Parents: This activity exercises memory. Call attention to the boy's clothes and the locations and shapes of the other items in the picture. Count down 20 seconds for your child.

Look carefully at the picture and try to remember what you see.
After 20 seconds, turn to the next page.

Let's Remember the Picture ②

To Parents: If your child struggles to find the differences, encourage her or him to go back to the previous page and start again.

GOOD JOB!
Sticker

Find 3 differences from the previous page.
Draw a ◯ around each one.

Let's Find the Picture Halves

To Parents: This activity builds spatial reasoning skills.

Look at the example pictures. If you cut the picture in the example in half along the white line, what will the 2 halves look like? Draw a ◯ around the 2 halves in the box on the right.

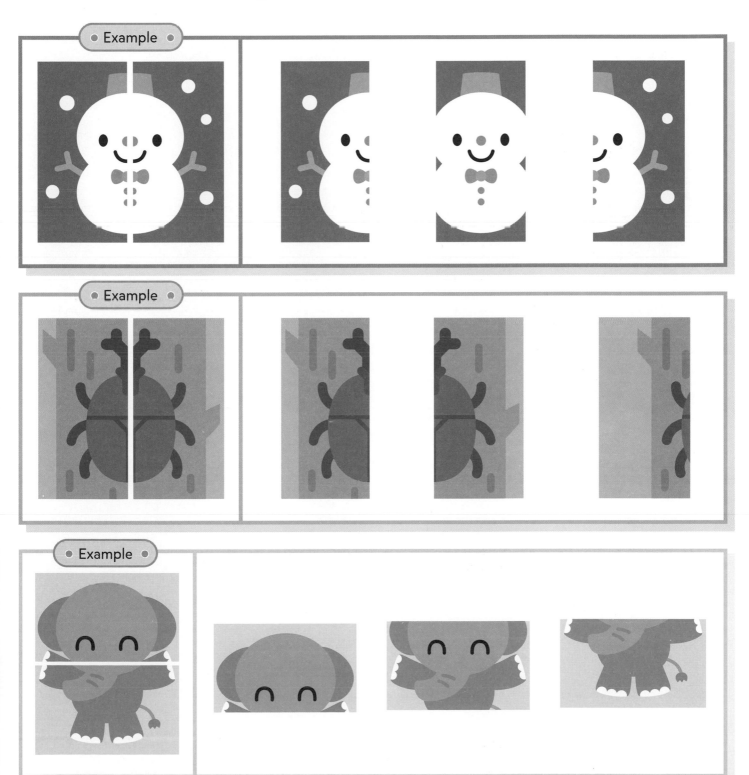

Let's Find the End of the Maze

To Parents: While doing this maze, your child will need to look ahead to avoid getting stuck in a dead end. The maze is based on the Cinderella story. After your child completes the maze, tell the story of Cinderella.

GOOD JOB!

Sticker

Draw a line from ➡ to ➡ to complete the maze.

GOOD JOB!
Sticker

Let's Find the Matching Shapes

To Parents: Here, your child will practice matching shapes. Call attention to the details of the shapes of the construction vehicles.

Cut out the cards at the bottom of the page.

Which vehicle matches each shadow? Glue each vehicle to its matching [ ].

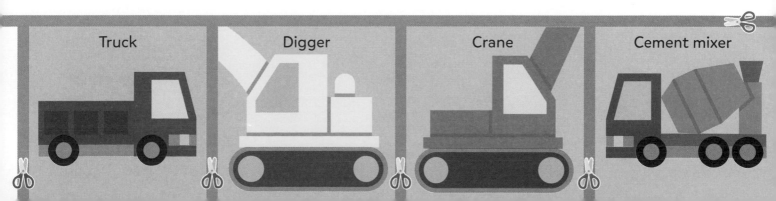

| Truck | Digger | Crane | Cement mixer |

48

Let's Find the Matching Shapes

To Parents: This activity challenges your child to find two shapes in each shadow. Be sure your child pays close attention to the details of each shape.

GOOD JOB!
Sticker

Each shadow below shows two objects together. Which objects are they? Color the ◯ under the objects that are part of the shadow.

Watermelon   Umbrella   Inner tube

Rake   Sunglasses   Shovel

Ice cream   Popsicle   Chocolate cake

Glue   Glue   Glue   Glue

Let's Spot the Differences

To Parents: Here, your child will compare similar images. If your child struggles to find the differences, offer guidance by asking about specific objects such as the clock or the items on the table.

Look at the two pictures.

Find the 4 differences in the bottom picture and draw a ◯ around each one.

Let's Find the Matching Sweets

To Parents: In this activity, your child will practice recognizing distinct objects within a group. Each plate of four desserts has an exact match. Guide your child to think of the four desserts as one set.

GOOD JOB!

Sticker

Find each set of 2 plates of desserts that is the same.

Draw a line to connect each matching plate.

Example

Let's Find Similar Objects

To Parents: This activity helps your child better understand the world. After your child finishes the exercise, ask him or her to tell you what jobs the other items do.

GOOD JOB!

Sticker

Find 3 objects that help with cleaning up.

Draw a ◯ around each.

Let's Find the Longest One

To Parents: Here, your child will practice comparing objects. Point out how all of the objects start in the same place to make it easier to compare their lengths.

Compare how long the 3 objects are in each box. Color **red** the ◯ next to the longest object and color **blue** the ◯ next to the shortest object.

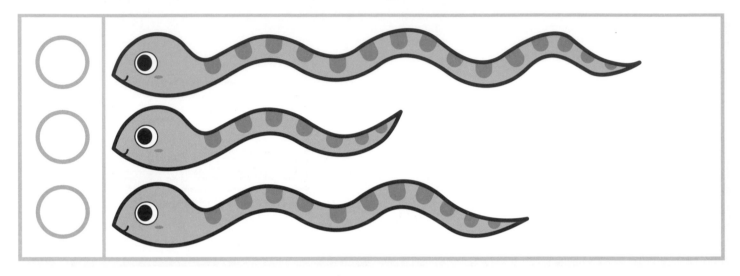

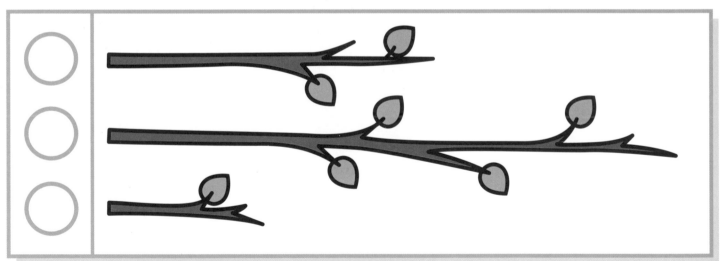

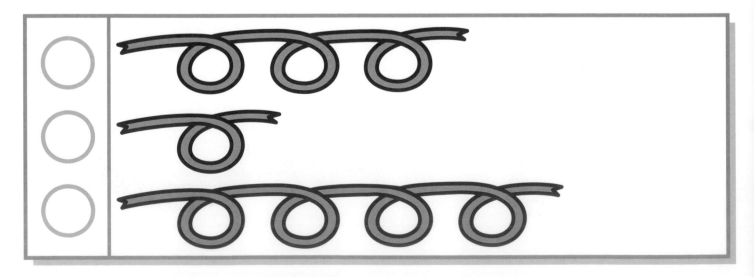

Let's Build a Picture

To Parents: This activity builds spatial reasoning skills. Call attention to the shape in the tree trunk and see if your child can show you different ways to arrange the triangles to make that shape.

GOOD JOB!
Sticker

Cut out the colored triangles below. Glue each triangle in place to make the same picture as in the example.

Example

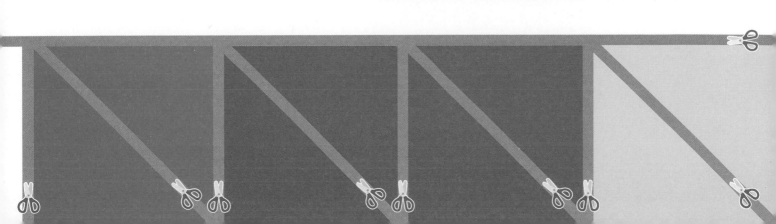

54

Let's Draw a Picture

To Parents: Drawing pictures encourages creativity. Be sure your child understands that the picture does not need to match the examples. When the drawing is done, ask your child, "What did you draw?" Compliment specific features of the drawing.

GOOD JOB!

Sticker

Draw a picture using the outline of your hand.

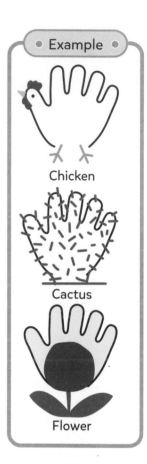

Example

Chicken

Cactus

Flower

How to Play

Place your right hand on the paper. Ask an adult to trace your hand. Then, draw anything you like using the shape of your hand.

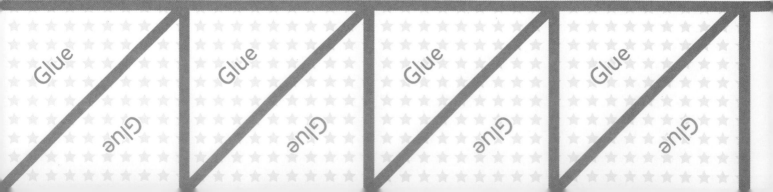

Glue Glue Glue Glue

Let's Group Similar Objects

To Parents: Here, your child will practice grouping similar items. This activity helps your child better understand the world.

Look at the foods and drinks in the [   ]. Which group below does each food or drink belong to? Put the sticker for each food or drink in its group.

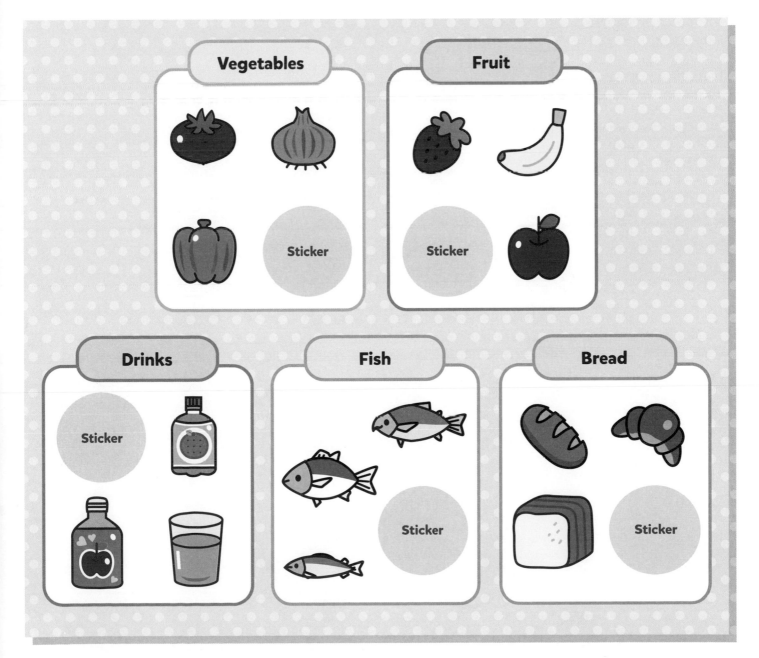

Let's Find the Perfect Matches

To Parents: The picture contains copies of the objects at the bottom of the page. It also contains some pictures that are not exact matches. If necessary, call attention to the colors and shapes of each hidden object to help your child.

GOOD JOB!
Sticker

Find the exact matches for the two boys, the inner tube, and the ship shown at the bottom of the page. Draw a line to connect each match.

Example

Let's Match the Animal Parts

To Parents: Here, your child will practice recognizing images from different views and connecting parts of a whole.

Draw a line to connect the animal's face to its tail.

Example

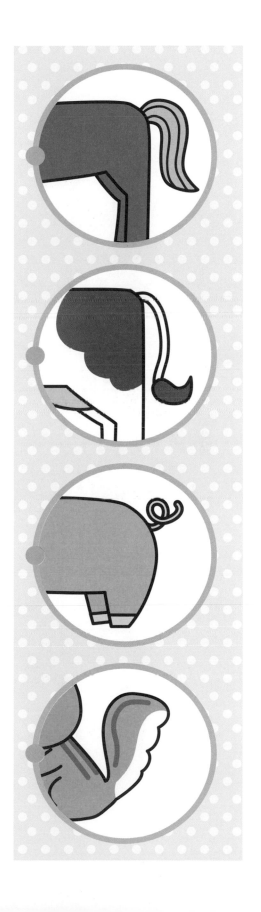

Let's Find the Matching Sundaes

To Parents: In this activity, your child will practice finding the differences among objects. Call attention to what's in each sundae, such as strawberries, bananas, or chocolate.

GOOD JOB!

Sticker

Find each pair of matching ice cream sundaes.

Draw a line between them.

Example

Let's Make Matching Flowers

To Parents: Your child will practice recognizing patterns by doing the activity below.

Put the  stickers on the flowers on the right to make them match the examples.

Let's Learn About Seasons

To Parents: This activity helps your child better understand the world. Start with the season your child understands best.

Find the picture on the right that matches the season on the left.
Draw a line to connect them.

Spring

Example

Summer

Fall

Winter

GOOD JOB!

Sticker

Let's Build a Picture

To Parents: This activity builds spatial reasoning skills. Have your child place the triangle pieces first and then glue them in place. The sailboat might be difficult for your child to complete.

Cut out the colored triangles below. Glue the triangles in the picture to make it match the example.

• Example •

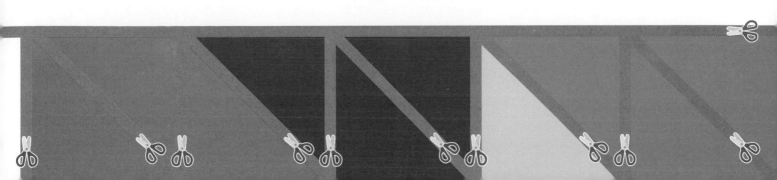

62

Let's Find the Perfect Matches

To Parents: In this exercise, your child will practice matching similar objects. Also ask your child to name each of the animals in the example boxes.

GOOD JOB!

Sticker

Which shape on the right matches the one in the example?
Draw a ◯ around it.

Answers for pp. 1–30

To Parents: These images show the answers to the activities. Use them to check the answers with your child.

p. 1

p. 2
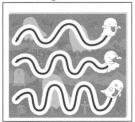

p. 3

p. 4

p. 5

p. 7
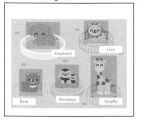

p. 8
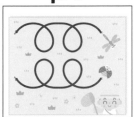

p. 9
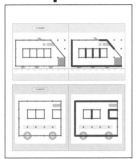

p. 10
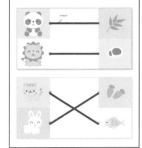

p. 11

p. 12

p. 13

p. 14

p. 15

pp. 17, 18

p. 19

p. 20

p. 21

p. 22

p. 25

p. 26

p. 27
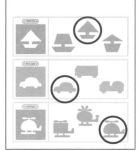

p. 28

p. 29

p. 30

*There are no answers for pages 6, 16, 23, and 24.

Answers for pp. 31–62

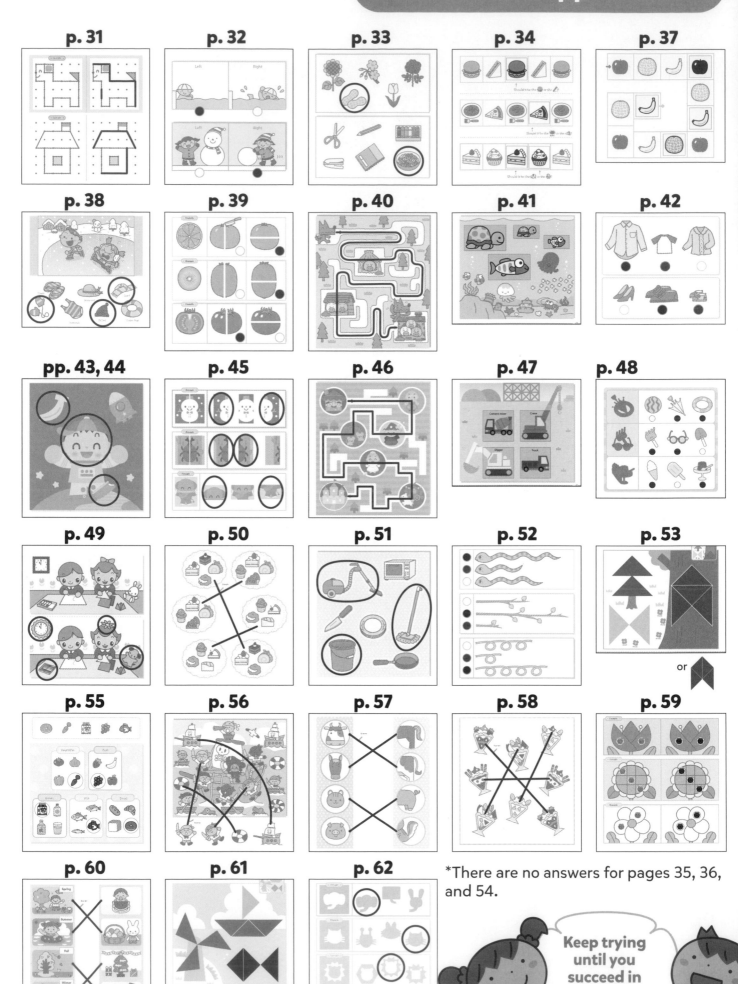

p. 31 **p. 32** **p. 33** **p. 34** **p. 37**

p. 38 **p. 39** **p. 40** **p. 41** **p. 42**

pp. 43, 44 **p. 45** **p. 46** **p. 47** **p. 48**

p. 49 **p. 50** **p. 51** **p. 52** **p. 53**

or

p. 55 **p. 56** **p. 57** **p. 58** **p. 59**

p. 60 **p. 61** **p. 62**

*There are no answers for pages 35, 36, and 54.

or

Keep trying until you succeed in each activity.

Game Board

You can draw and erase, again and again.

To Parents: Drawing encourages creativity. Have your child use water-based markers on the wipe-clean side of the board. Point out the patterns on the other fish if your child needs examples. When your child is finished, erase the board with a damp cloth.

Draw a pattern on the fish.

Let's Play!

To Parents: These activities build gross motor skills. Encourage your child to try them again and again to improve balance and get better at hopping on one foot and being a wheelbarrow.

How many times can you hop on one leg?

Hop using only one leg as many times as you can. Once both feet touch the floor, stop and ask your parent to tell you how many times you hopped.

How many steps can you take while being a wheelbarrow?

Ask a parent to hold your legs while you walk on your hands. Ask your parent to count how many steps you take.